The Open University

CW00726473

A103

AN INTRODUCTION TO
THE HUMANITIES

BLOCK 7

Looking Back, Looking Forward

This publication forms part of an Open University course A103 *An Introduction to the Humanities*. Details of this and other Open University courses can be obtained from The Call Centre, PO Box 724, The Open University, Milton Keynes MK7 6ZS, United Kingdom: tel. +44 (0)1908 653231, e-mail ces-gen@open.ac.uk

Alternatively, you may visit the Open University website at http://www.open.ac.uk where you can learn more about the wide range of courses and packs offered at all levels by the Open University

To purchase this publication or other components of Open University courses, contact Open University Worldwide Ltd, The Berrill Building, Walton Hall, Milton Keynes MK7 6AA, United Kingdom: tel. +44 (0)1908 858785; fax +44 (0)1908 858787; e-mail ouwenq@open.ac.uk; website http://www.ouw.co.uk

The Open University
Walton Hall, Milton Keynes
MK7 6AA

First published 1998. Reprinted 1998, 1999. Second edition 2000. Reprinted 2003

Copyright © 2000 The Open University

Edited, designed and typeset by The Open University

Printed and bound in the United Kingdom by Bath Press, Bath

ISBN 0 7492 8581 8

2.2

31611B/a103b7prei2.2

UNITS 31 AND 32 LOOKING BACK, LOOKING FORWARD

Compiled and written for the course team by Nora Tomlinson and Nigel Warburton

Contents

STUDY COMPONENTS				
Weeks of study	Texts	TV	AC	Set books
2	–	TV31 TV32	AC13	*The Arts Good Study Guide*

Aims

1 To provide an overview of the course.

2 To remind you of the key features of the eight disciplines which you have studied and of some of the links between them.

3 To provide you with a summary of the key points made in Units 1–30.

4 To provide some preliminary guidance on the revision and examination techniques which you will need as you progress in your studies with the Open University.

5 To encourage you to assess the skills you have acquired and developed while studying the course.

6 To suggest ways in which the knowledge and skills you have acquired while studying A103 can be carried forward to future studies.

1 INTRODUCTION

By now, you will have read all the main units of this course, written seven or eight TMAs and had an opportunity to write an assignment under something very similar to exam conditions, but that doesn't mean that you have finished the course. One of the most important aspects of any course you will take, whether with the Open University or elsewhere, is consolidation. When you were working through the units, you probably understood most of what you were reading, did some of the exercises, listened to the appropriate audio-cassettes and watched most of the television programmes. But now, after almost a year of study, can you recall all the things which you felt you had learned? You probably remember which units you liked best and which you liked least; indeed, you probably remember in quite some detail several of the units which really interested you. But can you remember the rest of the course? Probably not; most students are in this position. Remembering is always selective, and that very selectiveness can be an important learning process, since it establishes certain intellectual priorities which are bound to differ in some respects from one person to another. The Study Calendar allows two weeks for Block 7, but you will probably spend as much time on personal consolidation as on reading these units.

One way of measuring all that you have accomplished in the past year is to look back at the notes you made as you took stock of your learning process at the end of your work on the Preparatory Material (p.80). Compare your feelings then, and your assessment of your strengths and weaknesses as you embarked on A103, with all that you have achieved over the last thirty weeks. You will certainly know a great deal more than you did then, both about individual disciplines and about the ways in which these disciplines shed light on each other. And you should also feel more confident in your own powers of analysis, understanding, organization and writing, and if you move on to study at a higher level with the Open University, be better able to respond to the requirements of distance learning.

Part of the purpose of this block is to remind you of what you should take away with you from your study of the whole of this course. Obviously you can't be expected to remember absolutely everything you've covered; few of us would be capable of that sort of feat of memory. On the other hand, it would be a shame if six months from now your memories of A103 were just a blur, with no specific recollection of anything that you'd studied. You don't want to be in the position of having to read through all the units again to remind yourself of what you learnt. In many university courses, in the Open University and elsewhere, fear of having nothing to say in an exam acts as a spur to revision. A103 has no exam, so you might conclude that revision is irrelevant. However, it *is* relevant, not just so that you get the most you can from studying this course, but so that it genuinely fulfils its role of giving you a solid foundation on which to build your further academic studies. Revision – in the sense of an overview of the course you are now completing – should put the whole course in perspective for you. You may well find that looking back allows you to make sense of parts of the course which seemed obscure to you when you were studying them for the first time. But revision should also help you with future course choices, reminding you of the distinctive approaches of the different disciplines and of the different things you were able to learn from them.

This block contains a brief review of some of the most important points covered in the course, so it should help you to consolidate what you have already learnt. But it should also serve as a reference point if, later on in your studies, you need reminding of what the distinctive approach of a particular discipline is, or where in the course a particular method or technique was introduced. Remember that one of the central aims of this course has been to give you a solid foundation in the approaches of the different disciplines and to give you a sound basis for future course choices. At some later stage it may help you to refer to these units to check on what a particular discipline involves before making a decision about embarking on a course in a new discipline.

Another function of Block 7 is to give you a chance to step back from the details of the course and to get an overview of the route that you have travelled. When you were working on a particular unit, probably under time pressure, with a TMA looming, it may have been difficult to get a sense of its place in the block and in the course as a whole. This block allows you time to reflect on these wider issues.

Lastly, this block will give you some preliminary guidance on the sorts of revision and examination techniques you will need if you are going to take further courses in the Faculty of Arts.

So this block both looks back at what you have covered already and looks forward to how you might build on what you have already achieved.

2 THE EIGHT DISCIPLINES

One of the aims of A103 was to introduce each of the eight disciplines in the Arts Faculty, and you should now have a clear idea of some of their distinctive features. It is important to be clear about the distinctive qualities of these disciplines, both in content and in approach, particularly if you are going on to take further Arts courses with the Open University. Here are the eight disciplines, in the order in which they first appear in the course:

Art History
Literature
Music

Philosophy
Classical Studies
History
Religious Studies
History of Science

EXERCISE

Make some brief notes on each of these disciplines, in answer to the following questions:

1   What is distinctive about each discipline as an area of study?

2   What are its 'objects of study'?

3   What is the distinctive *methodology* of each discipline?

Be sure to write down something for each discipline before reading on.

DISCUSSION

You may have found this exercise quite challenging. While you were studying the units you were probably absorbed in the content of what you were working on, and may not have had time to reflect about the discipline within which you were studying. What follows are eight descriptions by members of the A103 Course Team of what they take to be distinctive about their discipline. Compare each one with your own notes made for the exercise above, and where there are differences, either of fact or of emphasis, look back to the appropriate unit where each discipline is introduced, to remind yourself what it deals with and how it is handled.

Course Team members' description of their disciplines

1   Art History (*Charles Harrison and Linda Walsh*)

The objects of study of Art History are explored through processes of seeing, touching and thinking, and through the exercise of imagination. They are made up of shapes and of colours and of physical materials such as canvas, paint, stone, wood, fabric and brick. These objects are varied in type: paintings, drawings, sculptures, buildings, monuments, installations, interior decoration, ceramics and so on. The main task of the Art Historian is to become fully acquainted with these objects, to establish meaningful relationships between them, to understand the historical circumstances in which they were produced and to explore particular methods of interpreting them. As with other areas of study, careful argument and use of evidence are essential to this process. However, the Art Historian faces the particular challenge of describing and discussing in verbal language objects which have powerful, non-verbal, visual aspects. One of the challenges in the study of art is to explain how objects may be seen to express emotions and ideas.

2 Literature (*Cicely Palser Havely*)

A literary text is an artefact made of words: it is something which has been crafted. Literary language tends to be more concentrated and patterned than everyday speech. Every word has a part to play and many words are deployed in ways which draw attention to their complex or wide-ranging significance or to their sound. Literary texts compress words and thoughts, often into highly patterned and structured forms which intensify their effects. Poetry is where this concentration of language is most intense, but in studying drama and the novel, you have also been shown how to focus your reading in order to get as much as possible from the language and form of the literary text.

As a discipline, literature traces what goes into a literary text by examining: (a) its place in the literary tradition; (b) the historical circumstances in which a text was produced; and (c) the particular circumstances of the writer. A careful reading of the text, together with a systematic consideration of these aspects, will take you a long way towards an interpretation of the literary work. There is no single right interpretation of a literary text, but a recognition of the strategies outlined above can help you to be objective in a field of study which is not primarily concerned with facts and certainties. As readers we, like all critics, are shaped by our own cultural and historical circumstances, by our previous reading (or lack of it) and by our own personal experience.

3 Music (*Fiona Richards*)

During your work on A103, you've looked at the building blocks of music, at the role of the listener, at music in performance and at music within a social and cultural context. As you've heard during the course, there is an enormous diversity of types of music, and of music's functions – music can be for entertainment and for self-expression; it can be part of religious ritual (TV15) or used in conjunction with drama (*Medea*). Despite these differences, all music has something in common, that is, it involves sound.

Pieces of music are made up of formal elements. These elements have been discussed throughout A103, and I hope that you are now much more familiar with rhythm, pitch, timbre and texture, and the ways in which these elements are manipulated, combined and organized within a musical structure. Sometimes these elements are manipulated for specific purposes, as in Richard Strauss's *Don Juan*, in which the composer's intention was to tell a story in music. But these elements alone are not the only crucial aspect of a piece of music. Most music involves a performer, or performers, and the performance environment can influence the effect of a piece of music; the South African music which you heard in TV10 is very successful as outdoor music, but would be much less effective in a concert hall. Music is also a cultural product, and different pieces of music are created according to the particular cultures from which they originate. Thus Hildegard of Bingen's unaccompanied vocal works were written for a specific purpose at a particular moment in time.

What you should take away from this course is some knowledge about the materials with which a composer works and an awareness of the reasons *why* certain sounds are chosen.

4 Philosophy (*Nigel Warburton*)

Philosophy is a subject which typically deals with very general issues about the meaning of life and the nature of reality. It puts a great emphasis on sound argument. The thinking skills acquired in studying philosophy are transferable to many other disciplines. The caricature of the philosopher as someone who is removed from real life isn't accurate. Philosophical problems are suggested by many aspects of our ordinary life. In TV4, for instance, you will have seen how abstract philosophical questions about the nature of individual freedom arose quite naturally from an examination of the debates about whether or not boxing should be banned. In other philosophy TV programmes Derek Matravers showed how the thoughts of the eighteenth-century philosopher Jean-Jacques Rousseau can contribute to present-day discussions about good government and the place of minority interest groups within a democracy.

Unlike many other Humanities disciplines, you have to do philosophy when you study it: you can't simply observe it from the sidelines. Studying philosophy requires an active and critical engagement with the ideas you study.

5 Classical Studies (*Phil Perkins*)

Classical Studies is the investigation of all aspects of Greece and Rome which were the predominant cultural forces in the region from Scotland to the Sahara and Spain to Syria between about 1000 BCE and 500 CE. It includes the study of ancient literature, art, politics, history, philosophy, society, artefacts, technology, cities, houses and people. This broad coverage enables the application of a diverse range of techniques and approaches, from literary and historical analysis to archaeological and art-historical investigation. The subject is distinctive in that it focuses upon a particular time period and geographical area rather than a single subject such as music or literature. However, the range of Classical Studies can be extended beyond the limits of the Greek and Roman worlds since classical culture has had a great influence upon the development of Western culture as a whole for at least the last five hundred years since the Renaissance. Therefore the study of the classical world can deepen our understanding of many concepts and aspects of contemporary society and culture, for example, of justice in your study of the Colosseum, of drama in your study of *Medea* or of imagery in your study of the paintings of David.

6 History (*Arthur Marwick*)

Unlike the other arts disciplines, History claims some methodological parallels with the natural sciences, though there are many differences: History is not basically a mathematical or an experimental subject. History is 'the study of the past' (not the past itself) and 'bodies of knowledge about the past', just as the natural sciences are studies of aspects of the natural world, and bodies of knowledge about the natural world. History is concerned with finding out about the past, with seeking out, collecting, selecting and organizing information. Historical study depends upon the specialized analysis of documents and all other kinds of primary source. The writing up of history, whether in a student essay or academic research paper or book, has to be tightly focused on a precise topic and calls for skills in identifying what is significant and in developing a clear balanced argument. These are all skills of great general utility. More broadly, History provides the knowledge of the past essential to the understanding of the present, and it provides a context for the historical study of art, literature, music, philosophy, religion and science.

7 Religious Studies (*Gwilym Beckerlegge*)

Having worked through the units on the study of religion, you will certainly know that practitioners of Religious Studies are determined not to be 'religious' in the way that they study religion! Unlike earlier theological approaches to the study of religion, Religious Studies is not founded upon assumptions about religious truth. Yet Religious Studies as a discipline is characterized by a working assumption that whether or not religion in any of its forms is true, religious belief and practice are sufficiently distinctive and important aspects of human life to warrant serious study. Religion has its public as well as private aspects and in Units 14–15, we looked at a number of ways in which an understanding of religion can help us to understand the world in which we live. Religious Studies has grown up beside a widening appreciation of how varied and complex expressions of religion can be. For this reason, Religious Studies encourages the study of different forms of religion and in ways that are sensitive to the different social and historical contexts of particular religions. In Units 14–15 and 28, we encountered examples of religions and new religious movements in Britain, India and the United States. While other disciplines in the Humanities and Social Sciences also devote attention to religion, this is often as part of a wider concern. For Religious Studies, the understanding of religion is its main concern, although we learn much besides in pursuing this goal, about our own assumptions and values and about societies the world over.

8 History of Science (*James Moore*)

History of Science starts from the premise that science is as much a product of human activity as anything studied in the Humanities. Our knowledge of nature has changed through time, as indeed have the individuals, the institutions, the instruments, and the practices by which it was created. Science therefore is historical and open to investigation by all the techniques used in History. Historians of Science have their own discipline simply because they are specialists. Like Art Historians, they study a large and technical subject, but with the same basic critical and analytic methods used by all academic interpreters of the past.

History of Science has no brief either for or against science. The discipline tries to explain where our knowledge of nature has come from, how it was formulated, and the processes by which some things have come to be credited as 'scientific' and others not. Because what counts as scientific keeps changing, Historians of Science do not limit themselves to subjects regarded as scientific or contributing to science today. They find the sources of science everywhere; nothing of human interest is ruled out. Science, past and present, is a cultural phenomenon. Understanding it brings into play the full range of skills required in studying the Humanities.

3 DISAGREEMENT AND TRUTH IN THE HUMANITIES

One aspect of this course which may have surprised you is the extent to which many Humanities subjects rely on interpretation. Unlike, say, arithmetic, where in most cases there is a definite right or wrong answer, in many Humanities subjects there is simply a hierarchy of possible interpretations, some better, some worse, but none having the status of 'the whole truth'.

In History, as Arthur Marwick has made clear, individual historians sometimes differ in their interpretation of evidence. Some historians like to present highly dramatic generalizations, such as Lawrence Stone and his thesis of the triumph of 'Affective Individualism' in the 1640s – a thesis which has been widely criticized by other historians of the family. Some historians have identified the family as primarily a 'patriarchal' institution, while others have stressed the important managerial role played by wives. Some historians have assigned a major role to the 'bourgeoisie' in bringing about the French Revolution, while others have argued that bourgeois figures were much keener to *become* aristocrats than to cut off the heads of members of the aristocracy. The point is that these disagreements are not simply for the sake of disagreement, but are part of the process moving towards the most accurate historical account.

In the study of literature interpretation requires a close attention to aspects of form. In asking of any work of literature, 'what does this mean?', we need to take account of how its language is organized. In studying poetry, this involves some awareness of the function of rhyme and rhythm, and even punctuation. So with literature, the question '*what* does it mean?' goes hand in hand with the question '*how* does it mean?' Stephen Regan pointed out that Shakespeare's Sonnet 18, 'Shall I compare thee to a summer's day?' appears to be addressed to a man, but we need to be careful about the way that information shapes our response to the poem. We also need to distinguish between Shakespeare the author and the speaker of the sonnet. Using the poem as evidence of Shakespeare's sexual preferences achieves little more than speculation, and tells us little, if anything, about how the poem works. The voice in the sonnet is constructed through language – scripted like an actor's role in a play - and any adequate interpretation of the poem requires some account of such devices as its strong use of repetition and its evocative imagery. Deciding whether the poem is addressed to a man or a woman does not in itself constitute an act of interpretation. What a poem means is always something much more than a summary of what it appears to be 'about'. As Unit 2 suggests (p.71), 'when language is working under pressure, especially in a tightly concentrated form such as the sonnet, the range of possible meanings is rich and diverse'. Literary criticism avoids suggesting that there is a single, verifiable meaning to be found in a poem, a play or a novel.

In Philosophy, we have considered Rousseau's arguments about the nature of democracy and their applicability to the present. When you listened to AC4, Band 2, 'Philosophy: Rousseau', you will have realized that there is still room for dispute about how Rousseau's ideas transfer to the present. Interpretation is involved. There is no simple, single answer to the questions raised by Rousseau's arguments, though there are many answers which are clearly wrong and can be shown to be wrong. For example, if someone declared that Rousseau in *The Social Contract* was arguing that the best approach to democracy is to rig the vote by devious means so that selfishly you get what you as an individual want, then it is quite easy to show by reference to Rousseau's text that this is absurd. Such an interpretation would have to ignore everything he had to say about the General Will. In Religious Studies, you will have noticed the scope for disagreement about what religion itself is. And so on.

Obviously not all matters are simply open to interpretation. The dates of the Second World War are not open to interpretation in the same way that the meaning of a Rothko painting is. However, as we have seen, historians can disagree over when the period of change conveniently referred to as the Sixties, or in Arthur Marwick's formulation, 'the long Sixties', began and ended. In the case of painting, the openness comes in part from the fact that the object in question is a work of art. Works of art are typically intended to be open to a range of interpretations, or are necessarily left open to a range of interpretations as a consequence of the very ways in which they establish their individuality. In those subjects which deal with works of art, such as Music, Literature and Art History and to some extent Classical Studies, you should by now have recognized that questions of meaning and interpretation are open-ended and cannot be decided once and for all.

Discovering the meaning of a painting is not like measuring the length of a piece of string. A painting of a cup is clearly not a painting of a dog. But while a given abstract painting may be quite unlike any other, it is much harder to pin down its meaning. There may be facts which you can discover about the artist's techniques and private life which provide an interesting basis for your interpretation, but they don't determine it in any straightforward way. This is one of the reasons why works of art can exercise our imaginations so profoundly.

These claims about the place of interpretation in the Humanities might seem to be heading towards the position known as *subjectivism*. This is the idea that every interpretation is as good as every other one; in other words, it's all just a matter of individual taste. But that is not what you have been taught in A103. In every example you've studied, some interpretations of evidence are better than others; some give a coherent explanation of available evidence, other don't. It would be absurd, for instance, to claim that *Pygmalion* is simply a moral fable about the dangers of elocution lessons, or that *Wide Sargasso Sea* makes a persuasive case for the re-introduction of slavery. But a subjectivist would have to say that these interpretations have equal status with the more orthodox ones. Again what needs to be emphasized is that in most Humanities subjects your first responsibility is to make a case for your interpretation and to provide compelling and reliable evidence in its support.

It is important to realize that just because many Humanities subjects rely on interpretations which are open to revision, this doesn't automatically make them vague, as, for example, some science students, used to dealing in what they think of as hard facts, might claim. In all the subjects that you have studied on this course, precision of observation and thought, careful use of evidence, and clarity of argument are essential to success. Just because you are giving an interpretation, it doesn't follow that this interpretation can't be clearly stated and the evidence for it presented in a convincing manner. Indeed, all progress in the Humanities relies on effective communication. Whether you are a student or a researcher you need to be able to present your conclusions in such a way that other people can appreciate the reasons and evidence you are providing in support of them.

 Finally, to complete your work on this section, you might like to re-read *The Arts Good Study Guide*, Chapter 6, section 3, 'Approaching analysis' and section 4, 'Interpreting meanings' which consider the relationship between analysis and interpretation. In particular, the Discussion box, 'Making meaning: 'anything goes'?', on page 204 is a valuable antidote to the subjectivism already discussed.

4 KEY POINTS FROM THE WHOLE COURSE

The third aim of this block is to provide you with a summary of the key points which are made in the written teaching material for the course. In order to present this in as brief and clear a way as possible, all course authors were asked the following question:

What do you consider to be the *three* most important points you want to get across in your unit(s)?

Their answers are given below, block by block and study week by study week. They are intended both as a kind of checklist against which you can measure your own understanding of the course, and as a guide to the kinds of issues which will be raised by other courses in the Arts Faculty which you may be considering for future studies.

Block 1   Form and Reading

Study Week 1 (*Charles Harrison*)

1   That art contains and embodies and expresses cognitively and historically significant material.

2   That understanding *how* it does so involves attention to the form, composition and techniques of individual works of art, rather than simply attention to what they illustrate.

3   That the kind of attention required can be learned and practised: its distinctive feature is the combination of rational enquiry and imagination. *Both* are needed.

Study Week 2 (*Stephen Regan*)

1   That poetry has a continuing value and importance.

2   That the sonnet has evolved as part of a tradition of writing and has altered in response to changing historical and political circumstances.

3   That literary criticism can enhance an understanding and appreciation of the creative possibilities of language.

Study Week 3 (*Fiona Richards*)

1   That music is made up of the formal elements of rhythm, pitch, timbre and texture.

2   That these elements are manipulated, combined and organized within a musical structure.

3   That musical performance involves composer, performer and listener.

Study Week 4 (*Nigel Warburton*)

1   That philosophy is an activity; you can't study philosophy passively.

2   That arguments are of great importance, and that they involve giving reasons for your conclusions rather than simply asserting them.

3   That reading philosophy is a skill which involves thinking critically about what is being read.

Block 2   The Colosseum

Study Week 5 (*Paula James*)

1   That culture of the classical period is relevant and accessible.

2   That studying classical culture in ways that recognize how it is both similar to and different from present-day Western civilization requires an informed approach and an integration of different types of evidence.

3   That a study of Roman society encourages an awareness of the attitudes and ideologies behind cultural practice.

Study Week 6 (*Colin Cunningham*)

1   That most buildings fit into traditions where both the forms and functions are partly governed by conventions and/or are developed by the freedom with which those conventions are handled.

2   That the classical orders of architecture are aspects of a system of designing that is relatively easy to analyse and which has been used by different architects in different ways for two millennia in the Western cultural tradition.

3   That the full meaning of architecture involves an understanding of its context, and that formal traditions are a part of that context.

Block 3   History, Classicism and Revolution

Study Weeks 8 and 9 (*Arthur Marwick*)

1   That history is knowledge about the past produced by historians; it is *not* the past itself.

2   That history is studied because what happened in the past has such importance for the present; societies *need* history.

3   That history is produced through the systematic analysis, involving certain methods and principles, of the relevant primary sources.

Study Weeks 10 and 11 (*Derek Matravers*)

1   That philosophy is not a subject which is made irrelevant by the fact that it is abstract; there are real problems for which people are prepared to die, which are basically philosophical problems.

2   That Rousseau's solution to the problem of legitimacy included each and every person at the cost of discouraging discussion and dissent.

3   That democracy allows discussion and dissent, but is unable to represent all our views equally, and some people's views do not get represented at all.

Study Week 12 (*Linda Walsh*)

1   That an investigation into the political, social and cultural circumstances in which a work of art was produced is a significant element of the viewer's interpretation.

2   That such an investigation must involve the careful selection and scrutiny of evidence.

3   That an historical investigation into a work of art is just as important in relation to formal and stylistic characteristics as it is with regard to content.

Block 4   Religion and Science in Context

Study Weeks 14 and 15 (*Gwilym Beckerlegge*)

1   That Religious Studies is founded upon assumptions about the long historical legacy and cultural breadth of religion that in turn is used as the basis for arguing for the development of a disinterested approach to the study of religion.

2   That the critical student of religion must think closely about how terms such as 'religion' and 'cult' are used and consider carefully and sensitively how well these concepts travel across cultures.

3   That establishing the boundaries of 'religion' is part of the study of religion, as is exploring diversity within this category. The importance of studying religion in context is emphasized.

Study Weeks 16 and 17 (*James Moore*)

1   That 'science' has a history; its meaning has changed through time. This history is the contingent outcome of *natural* human processes, with no overarching guarantee of 'progress'.

2   That what comes to be seen as true in science is to be explained in the same way as, or *symmetrically* with, what comes to be seen as false.

3   That History of Science as a discipline specializes in such explanations. Its resources are *contextual* rather than 'internal' or 'external' to the science of any period. The career of Alfred Russel Wallace (1823–1913) gives scope for writing History of Science in a *contextualist* way.

Block 5   Myths and Conventions

Study Week 19 (*Cicely Palser Havely*)

1   That drama, like the sonnet, is a form which has evolved from long traditions of both writing and performance.

2   That drama, like other literary forms (and indeed, other works of art), proceeds from a social and political context which it often challenges. *Pygmalion* challenges contemporary views on class and gender.

3   That, as with all literature, careful attention to the dramatic text is the basis for interpretation.

Study Weeks 20 and 21 (*Lorna Hardwick*)

1   That studying drama involves study of both text *and* performance.

2   That studying *Greek* drama involves awareness of both ancient and modern contexts and perspectives, including the mediating role of translation.

3   That studying *Medea* is both rewarding and disturbing.

Study Week 22 (*Fiona Richards*)

1   That composers work with the elements of music for particular expressive purposes.

2   That composers may attempt to depict or represent something 'extramusical' in musical terms.

3   That the composition and performance of music raise issues of gender.

Study Week 23 (*Cicely Palser Havely*)

1   That narrative forms have their traditions, and often rework familiar tales with a new twist.

2   That a complex novel, such as *Wide Sargasso Sea*, proceeds from, but also challenges the 'status quo' – here in respect of race and gender.

3   That to read a novel effectively, we must not only pay close attention to the text, but be aware of the difference between the context in which it was composed and the context in which we read it.

Block 6   The Sixties: Mainstream Culture and Counter-culture

Study Weeks 25 and 26 (*Arthur Marwick*)

1   That there is much more to the writing of history than might be thought; in particular, there are problems of periodization, explanation, strategy and structure.

2   That the Sixties is a period of great significance in social and cultural history and with respect to the themes of the course.

3   That the methods and principles of history can be applied to the Sixties; even if the historian has lived through the period, it is not good enough to rely on personal recollections.

Study Week 27 (*John Krige*)

1   That the science of the Sixties, no less than the other cultural products of the time, was strongly influenced by the rise of a pervasive counter-culture.

2   That the campaign for alternative science was, in part, generated from among the practitioners of mainstream science, so reinforcing the conclusion that Sixties counter-culture is not to be seen as completely separate from established mainstream culture.

3   That Sixties science was a characteristic product of the period in its demands for a more humane world, for a world whose peace and survival were not threatened by terrible scientific weapons of destruction, and a world in which women, no longer excluded from science, might promote its application for the benefit of humanity. For History of Science, the Sixties, like any other period, entails study of the society in which science was practised.

Study Week 28 (*Susan Mumm*)

1   That the relationship between the Sixties 'counter-culture' and religion is complex, variable and open to multiple interpretations.

2   That much of the literature relating to New Religious Movements and 'cults' is tendentious.

3   That religions originating in the Sixties have marked and still vigorous effects on our religious culture today.

Study Week 29 (*Fiona Richards and Trevor Herbert*)

1   That music is a cultural product, and that the three types of music considered in this unit, popular music, modern classical music and the Early Music Revival, need to be considered in the context of the Sixties in which they were produced.

2   That these three types of music can be considered in terms of an established culture and a counter-culture.

3   That in the Sixties, the Early Music Revival questioned and often contradicted the values that were most widespread in the world of classical music.

Study Week 30 (*Charles Harrison*)

1   That there are significant and interesting distinctions to be made between different forms of art in any given period.

2   That the nature of the conflict between socio-economic considerations and artistic interests has much to tell us about both.

3   That modern art can be understood and enjoyed.

5 CONNECTIONS BETWEEN PARTS OF THE COURSE

In a course as wide ranging as A103, which includes eight arts disciplines and which extends over many centuries, from classical Greece to the 1960s, it will not always be easy to retain a sense of the course as a coherent whole. This section identifies a number of key elements which contribute to the coherence of the course, and encourages you to explore aspects of these elements for yourself.

Methods of enquiry

The previous sections have shown you that while each of the eight disciplines is distinct, they share a number of common approaches.

EXERCISE

Think back over the course and your answers to question 3 in the exercise on page 7. Now make a list of the methods of enquiry which you think are shared by two or more disciplines, and then compare it with the list below. Together they should provide you with a summary of relevant methodologies to carry forward to future Arts courses.

DISCUSSION

1   The objects of study in Arts disciplines need to be placed in the historical and cultural context both of the period in which they were produced and the period in which they are being studied.

2   The careful study and analysis of primary source material is essential for the disciplines of History, Classical Studies, Religious Studies and History of Science.

3   Any study of the 'creative' disciplines of Literature, Art History and Music needs to take account of the crucial role of the imagination in the production and interpretation of works of art.

4   Any study of text-based disciplines, such as Philosophy or Literature, requires a very close and careful reading of these texts.

5   All the Arts disciplines rely upon interpretation and these interpretations need to be communicated clearly, and the evidence for them presented in a reliable and convincing manner.

Connections *within* disciplines

These are the easiest links to identify and are largely covered by the accounts of the eight disciplines by the course authors on pages 7–11. We would, however, like to suggest that you spend some time reflecting on your own experience and enjoyment of these links. How far, for example, did your viewing and interpretation of a painting by Rembrandt, which you studied in Study Week 1, illuminate your response to the painting of Rothko, which you studied in Study Week 30 and TV30, or your work on a sonnet by Shakespeare help you in your detailed reading of *Wide Sargasso Sea*?

Connections *between* disciplines

Many of these links are made explicit by the very structure of the course. Thus, for example, Block 1 addresses the concept of form with regard to different arts, and in Block 3, a grasp of some of Rousseau's ideas contributes to our understanding of the origins of the French Revolution. In Block 5, the concept of myth is used to explore the ways in which different disciplines rework traditional ideas, while Block 6, by focusing on a single decade of the twentieth century, the Sixties, shows how a study of several different disciplines can contribute towards understanding the culture of a particular period.

However, it may be that some of the more illuminating and thought-provoking connections have not been made explicit. What follows is an account of how some of these links have worked for *one* reader of the course. It is therefore necessarily personal and limited, but the intention is to encourage you to think about the connections which you have found as you have worked through the course; be prepared to annotate this discussion with your own examples.

Links with Art History

Some of these links are fairly obvious. Thus, for example, Linda Walsh's discussion of the paintings of David throws light on certain aspects of the French Revolution, and Charles Harrison's discussion of the paintings of Rothko illuminates certain aspects of the culture of the Sixties. However, there are other rather less obvious links. For example, the study of the Colosseum in Block 2 considers not only a building and the way it was used, but raises more general questions about the relationship between design and function. Additionally, the consideration of Roman artefacts as historical evidence for the functions of the Colosseum also provides us with the opportunity to consider other artefacts, such as ceramics or monuments, which might be considered to fall within the province of Art History, but which are not discussed under the Art History umbrella. Your work on Religious Studies has introduced you to a range of religious buildings and religious art and decoration, and while these were not the main focus of discussion in Block 4, your work on the relationship between form and meaning in paintings in Block 1 may have encouraged you to move beyond an awareness of the nature of religion itself to a consideration of the extent to which art and worship are linked.

Links with Literature

Again there are obvious links between Literature and Classical Studies in the extended work on *Medea* in Block 5, and between Literature and Music in the reworking of Hebridean myth by the composer, Judith Weir, as shown in TV22. Your work on songs in both Block 1 and Block 6 drew attention to the common patterning and lyric quality of poetry and music, while your work on *Medea* and *Pygmalion* will have revealed the performance element which drama shares not just with opera, but with religious ceremony and public spectacle. Both Literature and Philosophy are based on learning to read with great care and attention to detail, a skill which is valuable in the study of all arts disciplines.

Links with Music

Some of these have been discussed in the previous paragraph, though you may like to provide your own examples from the course – of music as spectacle, of music as an aspect of religious worship and of music used as narrative. Don't forget to reflect on the audio-visual components of the course as you do so. There is also a sense in which the concepts of musical texture and structure can inform our appreciation of other objects of study. It is possible, for example to speak of the visual patterning of the columns on the façade of buildings such as the Colosseum, or the patterned structure of a painting, as rhythmic.

Links with Philosophy

There is a sense in which Philosophy as a discipline pervades everything which you have done on the course, in that Philosophy encourages – indeed requires – an active engagement with the ideas you are studying, regardless of the discipline from which they derive. Additionally, the emphasis placed by Philosophy upon sound argument should have inculcated clear thinking and writing habits, which will stand you in good stead during the rest of your career as a university student. Philosophical ideas themselves pervade other disciplines. Your work on Rousseau in Block 3 has shown something of the dynamic which exists between revolution as a historical movement and democracy as a philosophical concept. We hope, too, that your work on philosophy will have suggested ways in which philosophical discussion can inform debates on the nature of religion, the existence of a divine being and the nature and function of science and technology in a modern democracy.

Links with Classical Studies

By its very nature Classical Studies is interdisciplinary, since it embraces Literature, Art, History, Religion and Philosophy. A103 has concentrated largely on the architectural, historical and literary aspects of Classical Studies, though we hope that your work on all these has shown you both the way in which Classical Studies can illuminate contemporary works of art, as well as showing you the difficulties of working with evidence which is rather more fragmentary than that which is available for other studies.

Links with History

History, like Philosophy, pervades every aspect of this course, since it provides the context for the study of the other seven disciplines. Without History as a study of the past, we would know little, for example, of the Greek civilization which produced *Medea*, little of the colonial background to *Wide Sargasso Sea*, or the improvements in navigational skills which made possible Wallace's early voyages of botanical discovery. In addition, History provides a training in the examination of evidence, the assembling of argument and the communication of ideas, and these skills transcend disciplines.

Links with Religious Studies

Like Classical Studies, Religious Studies is intrinsically interdisciplinary, and indeed cross-faculty, since it uses the disciplines of sociology as well as history. It has, as the objects of its study, religious writings, religious music, religious art and religious buildings, as well as the study of religious ideas and beliefs. Thus, for example, the sonnet, 'No worst, there is none' (*Resource Book 1*, A61) by the English Jesuit priest, Gerard Manley Hopkins, can be read as an example of poetry used to express intense personal emotion, but can also be placed in the context of the revival of the Roman Catholic church in England in the nineteenth century.

Links with History of Science

The closest links of History of Science are to History – indeed, it is part of History and employs an identical method of study. History of Science also has close links with Religious Studies, because the religious beliefs that, until relatively recently, have dominated societies include images of the cosmos, a type of intellectual construct that also lies at the very centre of science. While the images of the cosmos provided by science and religion do not inevitably conflict (great scientists of the past have been religious and priests have dedicated themselves to the scientific study of the world), confrontation has occurred, as in the challenge to orthodox Christian beliefs by nineteenth-century theories of evolution, discussed in Block 4. History of

Science is close to Religious Studies in another way: both disciplines, along with History, highlight the importance of avoiding bias. In Religious Studies, the integrity of study is shattered if other religions are viewed in the light of a favoured 'true' faith. Similarly, History of Science is undermined if the science of the past is viewed through the spectacles of present-day science, with its 'correct' perceptions, ignoring everything in the science of the past that it judged today to be 'wrong' or 'non-scientific'.

6 REVISION FOR EXAMINATIONS

One of the features of A103 is that it has no examination, although TMA 09 has been designed to provide you with the opportunity to write an assessed TMA under something approaching examination conditions, and to receive extended feedback on it. One of the implications of this policy is that you will move on to higher-level courses with no experience of a typical three-hour Open University examination. So it seems right that before you leave A103, you should spend some time thinking about the nature of examinations themselves.

EXERCISE

First of all, spend a few minutes noting down what seem to you to be some of the advantages and disadvantages of examinations.

DISCUSSION

Your list may have included the following:

Advantages

1   Examinations are a means of assessment which gives every student the same opportunities, and places every one on a level playing field. All students have the same length of time to complete the examination paper, unlike the amount of time devoted to an assignment, which can vary enormously according to individual circumstances.

2   Revision for examinations forces you to revisit much of the material in the course.

3   Examinations enable you to reveal your understanding of the *whole* course rather than the small part which is assessed by individual TMAs.

4   Course results, based on both continuous assessment and an examination, enable you to make a meaningful comparison with other students, both within the OU and at a national level.

Disadvantages

1   Examinations require you to work quickly and under pressure, and many students feel that they don't perform well in such circumstances.

2   Examinations often seem to be tests of memory as much as of understanding, and adult students often feel that their memories are no longer as reliable as they used to be.

3   Assignments can be written in familiar surroundings and, within the constraints of the cut-off date, to suit your own timetable. Examinations take place on a fixed date and at a fixed time and in a centre which may be some distance away; you may need to make a number of rearrangements of your private or professional life in order to attend.

4   Students receive no feedback from examinations, so they can learn nothing about how they may have gone wrong.

5   In Open University courses with an examination, half your course result depends on your performance for the three hours of the examination. You may be off-form on that day, though it is very unlikely that you would be off-form for every assignment.

Now read *The Arts Good Study Guide*, Chapter 7, section 1, 'Why exams?' (p.232) and section 2, 'Some myths about exams' (p.234). Are the reasons given as a justification for exams the same as your own? Are the myths about exams the same as the disadvantages which you have just listed? Where there were differences of opinion, think hard about your own reasons and about those given in *The Arts Good Study Guide* and see how far these differences can be reconciled.

You won't need the rest of the detailed advice in Chapter 7 of *The Arts Good Study Guide* this year, so you may simply like to skim through the remaining sections so that you have an idea of the advice which will be available to you in future years. You may also be reassured to know that the OU does provide a great deal of help for its students to ensure that you are not disadvantaged in any way. Below are some of the most common queries about OU exams, together with the official, and we hope, reassuring answers.

1   *Q.* 'I've had a terrible year – illness, divorce, death in the family, TMAs lost in the post ... Will the Exam Board take this into account?'

A. You can tell the Exam Board about problems during the year using a form which you can request from your Regional Centre. Only serious circumstances will be taken into account.

2   *Q.* 'My exam was a fiasco. I was late because I was involved in an accident, my train was cancelled. I felt ill ... Can I tell anyone?'

A. Fill in the form in your Exam Booklet. This can also be used to cover problems during the revision period.

3 *Q.* 'I am too ill to take the exam, my baby is due three days before the exam ... What do I do?'

A. You may qualify to take a special exam. Contact your Regional Centre Exams Section *within seven days* of the exam, providing evidence.

4 *Q.* 'The exam is still some way off, but I know my employers are going to send me overseas.'

A. Exams can be arranged overseas with sufficient notice; usually you need to ask by mid-August. Contact the Exams Team in your Regional Centre. If you have insufficient notice you may qualify for a special exam – see Question 3 above. Note that if you are a student based in Europe, your examination will be arranged in your country of residence.

5 *Q.* 'I can't get time off work.'

A. If your employer can't release you on a particular day, contact your Regional Centre Exams Section. If you can provide confirmation from your employer, you may qualify for a special exam.

6 *Q.* 'I'm disabled. Is there any help in the exam?'

A. Whether the disability is permanent or temporary, we try very hard to help. For example, we can organize:

extra writing time	taped papers
rest breaks	enlarged or Braille papers
home exams	enlarged diagrams
an amanuensis	the use of word processors

Please ask for help but give the Exams Section in your Regional Centre as much notice as possible. If it's too late for us to help, you should use the form as in 2 above.

7 *Q.* 'I get totally stressed out by exams and I just don't do as well as I might.'

A. Some Regional Centres provide exam counselling; contact a Senior Counsellor or Regional Adviser at your Regional Centre.

8 *Q.* 'I could really do with some help with revision and exam technique.'

A. Read Chapter 7 of *The Arts Good Study Guide*! Your tutor may also be able to help; ask him or her to request a special session for you. Your Regional Centre may put on an Exams workshop.

Remember that revision is part of the process you have been undertaking as you have worked through this block. What you will need to add to this for future courses is the examination itself, and we hope that you are reassured that The Open University examination system is designed to cope with the needs of adult learners. You might like to make a note to refer to this section of Block 7 at this time *next* year when you may, in fact, be preparing for an exam.

7 TRANSFERABLE STUDY SKILLS

Please have *The Arts Good Study Guide* to hand as you work through this section.

So far in this block, we have been concerned largely with revision of knowledge and understanding, by considering the characteristics of each discipline as well as themes, issues and methodologies which provide links throughout A103. But in addition to this knowledge and understanding which you have gained, you will also have acquired and improved a whole range of study skills. Some of these are basic skills, such as close reading and essay writing, needed in the study of all disciplines, while others, such as the ability to analyse a poem, or a painting, are more discipline-specific skills. What follows is a list of the skills which we hope you will have acquired and improved during the last twelve months. Cast your eye over this list, treating it rather as you would a piece of market research, and award yourself points for what you feel represents your achievement in each of these skills. Use a scale of 1 to 10, where 1 equals a poor achievement and 10 equals brilliant. Don't be modest about this! You may not feel that you can award yourself 10 points for everything on this list, but it should provide a measure of the improvements which you have made.

Study skills	Score
gaining pleasure from learning	10
reading academic texts, such as course units, articles or books with understanding	9
analysing aural texts: music, whether recorded or in live performance audio-cassettes containing poetry or play readings or talks on some aspect of the course	9
analysing visual texts: paintings buildings artefacts television programmes stage performances of dramatic texts	10

Study skills	Score

analysing written texts:
philosophical arguments
historical primary sources
literary works, such as poems, plays and novels | 10 |

making notes on:
key points from course units and other academic texts
key points from audio-visual material
key points from lectures or discussion
notes for assignments | 8 |

organizing, filing and retrieving notes and other course material | 9 |

planning and writing TMAs, including revising your own written work critically before submission | 9 |

absorbing criticism in the light of feedback | 10 |

taking part in group discussion:
tutorials
self-help groups | 10 |

using telephone/computer e-mail to contact your tutor or other students | 0 |

study time management:
keeping to the course Study Calendar and TMA cut-off dates
balancing the demands of the course with the demands of your personal and professional life | 10 |

confidence in your own ability as an independent distance learner | 8 |

We are not going to suggest any kind of ideal total score! Apart from anything else, not all the points will apply to all students: you may have, for example, chosen not to use e-mail. But we hope the activity reassured you about how far you have travelled since you began the course 32 weeks ago, though you may feel that you could make an even greater improvement in some areas; most of the skills are 'core' skills, which will be important, whatever you plan to study next. AC13, Side 1, records the views and experiences of a small group of students who have completed an Arts Foundation Course, and you may like to compare their views with your own. Remember that *The Arts Good Study Guide* covers all the skills in the list above, and that between now and the start of your next course, you could usefully use its index to find those areas where your score was not as high as you would have liked, and follow the advice which is given in the relevant section. Additionally, the course units are indexed, so you can easily locate those parts of the teaching material which deal with subject-specific skills which you feel may need honing before you start your next course.

8 CONCLUSION

The end of A103 is a good time for you to stop and take stock of how well you think you have coped with the additional demands which A103 has imposed on your life and what you can do to improve your organizational efficiency in the future. We hope that working through this last block has enabled you to draw up a kind of balance sheet of your achievements, and that as you move on to other courses, you feel you are well in credit! You have now completed an Arts course at undergraduate level and should feel confident that you can move on to second-level courses, whether you choose a single discipline or an interdisciplinary course. The whole of the A103 Course Team offers its very best wishes to you in whatever studies you undertake in the future.